WEAPONS OF MASS
CONSTRUCTION

1ST EDITION

UNVEILING HUMAN POWER,
ONE THOUGHT AT A TIME

SHANTELL

WEAPONS OF MASS CONSTRUCTION

1ST EDITION:UNVEILING HUMAN POWER,
ONE THOUGHT AT A TIME

S H A N T E L L

Published in the United States of America

ISBN: 978-1-961392-52-6
Body, Mind & Spirit / General
16.06.21

CONTENTS

INTU

I've often sensed things, but the things that I'd sensed seemed logically out of the way; only to manifest shortly after, just as my mind envisioned. Now in my mature mental degree, I actually *know* that senses are more accurate than my visual interpretation of them. The worst thing I've done was to second-guess my senses with someone else's who'd opposed it and I followed, since it was logical to do so. What a blunder! Now my senses and I are one and other's input on our oneness is void.

Furthermore, my urgings are personal and not open for reasoning, criticism, or debate of any sort due to it being mine, and my hinting toward its uniqueness is often misunderstood or perceived in a negative light. So in order to preserve my previous *mind energy* (*WOMC* Volume 2), I've learned to avoid defending, explaining, and/or advertising what is designated and divinely sacred for me or for you—if you can relate.

INTU
Elaboration: INTU

"Good morning, sir."
"Good morning to you too."
The two men greeted each other in passing, basically acknowledging each other's presence. It was somewhat inevitable due to one of the men working as a janitor in the train station and the other being a frequent commuter.

"I get good vibes from that man," the janitor internally noted.

The train station was very crowded on that particular morning due to a cat cashing out on all nine of his lives on the live electric rail.

"*Aww man. Imma be late!*" the commuter said out loud.

Everyone within earshot turned around to get a visual of the one who dared to express what they themselves were thinking.

The commuter was so caught up in his own thoughts that he ignored all the attention that was directed at him and simply retrieved the book he was reading for his commute to and from work. The book that had him look deeper into himself as well as his self-worth was titled: *No Problems, Just Situations and Solutions!* by Michael Price.

"This is crazy!" Twenty minutes passed by and the commuter started to become aggravated. He resumed reading the book, losing track of time until he was disturbed by that sound of a Latina woman's voice.

"This is not good for me, *conyo!*"

The commuter became frustrated.

"No train yet!" he softly whispered to himself.

Out of nowhere, a strong urge overcame him, and the commuter began to see the situation from a different perspective. He began having visions of the comfort of his apartment and it became the focal point of his pondering. A sudden impulse to call in strongly emerged. At first, the commuter rejected the thought due to it being out of character and out of his comfort zone, but the sense was extremely powerful. Hesitantly, he walked up a flight of steps from the subway's platform.

As he approached the main level, the commuter questioned himself, "Why am I doing this?" He shook it off and continued to the exit.

"Forgot something, sir? the Janitor inquired.

"No, sir. It's funny you asked because I just got a strong urge to go back home today," the commuter responded in a tranquil tone.

"Are you sure that you are not getting impatient?" the Janitor asked sarcastically.

At this point, the commuter became frustrated because he found himself explaining himself to a stranger. "No, sir! Uh…have a great day!"

The commuter made it to his apartment in several minutes. He immediately plopped down on his sofa and fell into a deep sleep only to be awaked by the constant ringing of the landline phone.

"Oh no! I forgot the callout hotline!" The commuter grudgingly lifted the receiver. "Hello?"

"Oh my God! Thank you, Jesus! Thank you, thank you so much!"

"Mom? Hello? What is going on? Why are you crying?"

"Thank you, Jesus, for keeping my son alive, Thank you so much! Oh my God! Son, two planes just crashed into your workplace and both buildings collapsed. So many people have died."

YOU KNOW BETTER

When the subconscious is stimulated, we are made aware of the file that is being pushed into our consciousness, and it is at that point we must take heed and respond to ourselves in accordance with the file or reminder.

The acronym YKB, which stands for You Know Better, can be paralleled with our gut feelings except the gut feelings are not a direct reminder, but more of an indirect reminder from our thoughts. In many cases, those gut feelings are simply triggers from the S-Conscious that pushes the file to the conscious mind or our regular thought pattern. At this point, we become aware of a sense, an urge, or a feeling. Once we become aware, it is our duty to interact accordingly or we will pay the penalty of regret or whatever else that results from going against the grain of the natural order of existence. So if it's the gut feeling or the direct sensors from the S-Conscious, you acknowledge your power. Don't betray yourself when it comes, use it or you will lose it.

Does this sound familiar? Has there ever been a moment when you felt something and went against your senses, urges, and/or feelings only regret it? Well, let's amend your super memory bank by attaching a file to the memory of regret and acknowledging that you simply did not know any better.

Wisdom comes at a price. Therefore, when we get those senses and urges, we now know we are not going crazy or just having anxiety. We now *know* and understand that they are linked to our oneness with all of existence. We know better, so let's do better!

Take a second write down how this lesson resonates within you by writing a scenario from your past or someone else's.

_____
_____
_____
_____
_____
_____
_____
_____
_____
_____
_____
_____
_____
_____
_____
_____
_____
_____
_____
_____
_____
_____

_____
_____
_____
_____
_____
_____
_____
_____
_____
_____
_____
_____
_____
_____
_____
_____
_____
_____
_____
_____
_____
_____
_____
_____
_____
_____

_____
_____
_____
_____
_____
_____
_____
_____
_____
_____
_____
_____
_____
_____
_____
_____
_____
_____
_____
_____
_____
_____
_____
_____
_____
_____

_____
_____
_____
_____
_____
_____
_____
_____
_____
_____
_____
_____
_____
_____
_____
_____
_____
_____
_____
_____
_____
_____
_____
_____
_____

ACCORDINGLY

Why do we put our left shoe on our right foot? Actually, most of us don't. We put our left shoe on our left foot and the right on the right because that is how they were designed to fit our feet. I'm not saying that we can't put our left shoe on our right foot; but I am saying that if we do, it would not be in accordance with how they are designed and it will cause us suffering and pain of some degree.

If we deal with the other parts of our lives *accordingly* with this thought pattern, life would be like putting the correct shoe on the correct foot on the correct shoes. It is way more comfortable. Therefore, when we deal with people, places, things, situations, and circumstance in accordance with nature, we actually enhance our lives by diminishing needless suffering ignited by our desires, perceptions, and attitudes toward life in general. How, you ask? Sometimes I get upset when things do not turn out the way I expected them to or how I wanted them to be. When I become conscious of my reckless thinking, I immediately redirect my thought pattern. This is only possible because of my perception of a word that has existed long before I was physically created, accordingly.

Furthermore, when life is not going the way I want it to or just seems as if it's out of whack, I stop then ask myself, "Am I operating in accordance with how I want things to be? Are my shoes on the right feet?" For instance, people have come to despise me in my travels without even getting the chance to know me. Now naturally, it bothered me at first because I can't understand how people could do that. Yet I have learned to let them be as they are because they are actually in accordance with nature, and if I forced myself on these people, it will only get worse because they will not appreciate me. To make a short story shorter, I have found it in my best interest to deal with those people accordingly from moment to moment, which became a basic formula to maintain peace of mind.

Short Demonstration: Accordingly

"Good evening, big brother. How are you? Do you have time to talk?"

"Sure, I always have time for my Little Brother. What is going on?"

"I really don't understand what's going on with my girlfriend and I. When we first met it, was all smiles and laughs, but now it seems as if we primarily shout and frown."

"What do you mean *shout and frown?*"

"When I say *shout and frown*, I mean bickering and fussing over everything."

"That sounds like the most normal relationship to me."

"I thought a normal relationship was peace and harmony, smiles and cheers."

"Man, you better wake up! Most relationships go through this stage. Actually, all of life goes through stages of chaos and order. If you think about it, the sun rises in the early morning, reaches its peak around noon*ish*, starts to descend in the evening, then we have night. This cycle is completed over and over, seemingly forever."

"What does that have to do with me and my girlfriend?"

"Well, if you look at this situation from a broader perspective, you will see that your relationship is just going through a cycle. It will leave that cycle and enter another, then another, parallel to the binary system in the digital world."

"So what am I supposed to do? Just live in strife and create a dysfunctional union?"

"No, bro! That is not what I'm saying. What I am saying is, find a way to get though each cycle or season as you do in all other areas of life. For instance, how do you dress in the winter?"

"I wear warm clothing."

"That is exactly what I was thinking! Now when summer comes, how do you dress?"

"I dress lighter because it gets very hot, but I don't understand how this pertains to my situation."

"The point simply is that you dress heavily when it's cold and dress lightly when it's hot. Basically, you're dealing with each season accordingly and don't fuss with winter or with summer. You simply adapt. Now if you did the same in your relationship, you would see how dealing with life in accordance with its nature would bring you that peace and harmony that you desire, because it comes from you!"

"Wow! I never looked at it from that perspective."

"I have to go, but please stay positive, brother."

"Hold on. How can I go about dealing with my girlfriend accordingly?"

"That, my brother, is solely on you and your intentions for your relationship. I trust that your ingenuity and discretion will guide you accordingly.

I-REALITY AND REALITY

In your opinion, is *truth* a *fact* or is *fact* an essential element of the *truth*? I'll agree with *fact* as being an essential element of the *truth* and the *truth* being in conformity with the *facts*, which equates to reality. *Fact* can be truth in its purest form, which equates to reality. Yet *fact* can be twisted to fit the perception and imagination of a group or individual (i.e. *I*-reality). *I*-reality is an individual's perception, while reality is the truth in its purest form.

Therefore, we must be conscious of the difference between *I*-realty or reality. How? By constantly evaluating the facts and our perceptions and then deciphering the truth.

Take moment to write and explain how this lesson resonates in your thought pattern and how it can be productive to you in the future.

_____

_____

_____

_____

_____

_____

_____

_____

_____

_____

_____

_____

_____

_____

_____

_____

_____

_____

_____

_____

_____

_____

_____

_____
_____
_____
_____
_____
_____
_____
_____
_____
_____
_____
_____
_____
_____
_____
_____
_____
_____
_____
_____
_____
_____
_____

_____
_____
_____
_____
_____
_____
_____
_____
_____
_____
_____
_____
_____
_____
_____
_____
_____
_____
_____
_____
_____
_____
_____
_____
_____
_____

_____

_____

_____

_____

_____

_____

_____

_____

_____

_____

_____

_____

_____

_____

_____

_____

_____

_____

_____

_____

_____

_____

_____

_____

_____

_____

GOLD DIGGING

When digging for gold, miners must mentally look past the dirt and other natural elements in order to obtain what they are looking for. The gold is actually part of that dirt and other natural elements; but it's just the gold that is being sought after, not the dirt.

Like gold miners, we, too, will find that it is in our best interest to sift through life for gold (peace) as an objective and not become blinded by the dirt and the rocks (rough times) that are actually part of a package with the gold (good times). In other words, hard times and not-so-peaceful situations in life should be embraced in order to find the gold or peace inward and outward.

If that relationship is important to you, stop looking at the *rocks and dirt*, be like the gold miners and keep looking for that *gold*. If that job is that important to you, look past that bitter manager and look for that *gold*.

Short Demonstration: Gold Digging

"Good morning, boss."

"What's so good about it?"

"We are alive, for starters."

"So let me ask you a question. Does that apply to the people who are suffering from cancer, in pain from pain of chemo, and in agony from the mental strain that life has dealt them?"

"Technically, yes. I would think they have a fighting chance. But I also get your point, boss."

"Oh, you do, huh?"

"Yes, I do. I also respect your stance."

"How did you develop your stance?"

"From being a very pessimistic person long ago"

"No way!"

"Yes. That is why I can empathize with you."

"I may make a nice living, drive a nice car, live in a nice house, but the truth of the matter is, I have plenty of issues. I often feel as if life is a totally negative experience, and that is the way it is going to be."

"Once again, I empathize and also respect your stance."

"You said that already! So you think I am a miser?"

"No, sir."

"Yes, you do. I can tell! You can be real with me, you know."

"I am being as real as reality permits me to be, sir. It's just that I have been where you are and I don't judge you, but I actually understand that it will take time for you to reverse your views about life. I remember how I wanted to be happy. I wanted to be at peace but I didn't know how. But now I do! I'm the only one who could change my mind. People could talk till their throats get dry, but it still would be me who will make the change."

"I want to be happy, I want to be at peace but things keep happening, and I keep getting more stress now it simply has become the norm. So I accept it!"

"Let me ask you a question. Does a gold mine obtain gold?"

"Yes, of course!"

"If we were to walk into a gold mine and start digging, what are the chances of us finding gold after digging for ten minutes?"

"To be honest, I don't know. But my guess would be that we will not find a penny's weight of the precious metal, because that takes time and work. I guess that the time we put in in would determine our success or our failure."

"Do yourself a favor and apply the same principle to finding your peace in the gold mine called life."

"What do you mean by that?"

"You said that you wanted peace and then you said that the time that we put into something determines our success or failure, so go on gold digging for the peace that you desire."

"You witty son of a gun! Get out of my office, and thanks for the insight. Now get to work!"

THANK YOU

Thank you for loving me so...

Today I assess life by counting my blessings as opposed to my so-called curses. Although I have plenty that I can complain about, I choose not to gripe about the undesirable of life because they play their part for the greater good.

I claim my victory, and I know and understand that feelings derive from thoughts, and although my feelings are sometimes uncontrollable, my thoughts are...paradox huh? Therefore, I give thanks to for all the things, people, places, situations, and circumstances due to them all being founded in our essence.

If I complain verbally or mentally, I will be creating feelings in accordance with my thoughts that will cause many hardships in my life. Instead, I'd rather create a fertile ground for seeds of peace to be planted, cultivated, and harvested. Moreover, I've learned that I sow situations from my thoughts. This is why I'm appreciative of all things and I seek peace in the midst of mayhem, which, to me, is seeking peace in all things.

Please write and explain what you are grateful for and who you give thanks to.

_____

_____

_____

_____

_____

_____

_____

_____

_____

_____

_____

_____

_____

_____

_____

_____

_____

_____

_____

_____

_____

_____

_____

_____
_____
_____
_____
_____
_____
_____
_____
_____
_____
_____
_____
_____
_____
_____
_____
_____
_____
_____
_____
_____
_____
_____
_____
_____
_____

_____
_____
_____
_____
_____
_____
_____
_____
_____
_____
_____
_____
_____
_____
_____
_____
_____
_____
_____
_____
_____
_____
_____
_____

THE PROCESS

Once I acknowledged something, someone, or a particular place to be in the process of manifesting itself as being a foe. I find it in my best interest to take steps in the direction of securing myself.

I secure myself by first knowing that nothing happens overnight, so that I can have patience with the seeds that I must plant. When I place a thought into my memory bank, it alerts my consciousness of the danger that lay ahead if I continue to allow momentum to build. From this point, my subconscious places up caution signs every time my consciousness ventures over to danger zone and reminds me of the danger that is lurking.

WEAPONS OF MASS CONSTRUCTION

Short Demonstrations: The Process

"Mom, why are you calling me this late at night? It's actually 4 a.m."

"Because I am your mom, and I am just checking on you to make sure that you are okay since you did not call before you went to bed last night, as you promised."

"Mom, I'm eighteen now and away in college. You have to trust me."

"Trust you, young lady? I love you, and I will call as often as I please. You are going to have to deal with it! I pay for your education so that you will do well. I am protecting my investment."

"I love you too, Mom. I'm super grateful for ensuring that I get this education, but you have to respect me and have some faith in me."

"Are you sassing me, young lady?"

"No, ma'am. I will never! However, I am trying to communicate with you, just as you taught me to do with everyone else when there seems to be a miscommunication."

"Miscommunication?"

"Yes, Mom. This is a miscommunication because you are treating me as if I am thirteen years old?"

"Young lady, I respect you and treat you as the age that you are, but you are still my child and will always be."

"Yes, Mom, I will always be your daughter, but a child I am no more. Thanks to you, I'm away in school as training to become a responsible adult. Thank you so much, Mom."

"You are welcome, baby! See, you do understand."

"Yes, I do, Mom. But you have missed my point."

"Did I?"

"Yes, Mom. I am not a child anymore. I am growing up and will continue to grow up. After college, I will fully provide for myself, have my own place, maybe get married, and have children one day—but not anytime soon though."

"Please forgive me. I know, baby, I know. I apologize. I just have to get use to you being on your own. I guess it's just a *process*."

DARK MOMENTS

Moments describe time, time measures space, and space is basically an indescribable motion. Moments will change, but we may maintain a positive perception of life in general *if* we choose to. Yes, we do have a choice; but the question is whether we will *enforce* it or not?

Dark moments are times when we can exercise the spiritual wisdom from our perspective sources, whether it is the church, mosque, temple, synagogue, or some other spiritual source. Regardless of what our religion is, we have the power to see our darkest moments as a chance to transform them into our most enlightened moments: intu-accordingly-gold digging the process.

Take a moment and write how you can transform your darkest moments into your most enlightened moments via the four previous weapons of mass construction (WOMC).

_____

_____

_____

_____

_____

_____

_____

_____

_____

_____

_____

_____

_____

_____

_____

_____

_____

_____

_____

_____

_____

_____

_____
_____
_____
_____
_____
_____
_____
_____
_____
_____
_____
_____
_____
_____
_____
_____
_____
_____
_____
_____
_____
_____
_____
_____
_____

_____
_____
_____
_____
_____
_____
_____
_____
_____
_____
_____
_____
_____
_____
_____
_____
_____
_____
_____
_____
_____
_____
_____
_____
_____

NATURE'S COURSE

In some instances, it's best to let a person, place, thing, circumstance, and/or situation remain as it is. By letting nature take its course, we will then get more knowledge and understanding out of the subject. Yet the more we try to change a subject (person, place, thing, circumstance, and/or situation) via some sort of manipulation, we actually oppose reality. Therefore, accept or reject the *subjects* for what they are naturally made up of, because anything else is a seed of trouble. Moreover, to force your left shoe on your right foot is to oppose nature.

An attempt to turn summer into winter is futile. Why? On its own, winter will run its course naturally then spring will emerge and run its course, making way for the summer. To try and control this process would be extremely destructive to one's self as well as the foundation from which the seasons derive. That unwritten law applies also to people, places, things, circumstances, and situations. Therefore, it in our best interest to allow nature to take its course by dealing with it accordingly, despite how we feel or think. Then we will reap the peace of this beautiful life. For instance, if you are not in the mood to speak to someone, you should not speak with them, unless it is of vital importance to do so. If you do speak but don't want to, you may be opposing nature and come to regret it later. The same goes for performing a certain task; if it is forced, it may be the cause of regret later on. Nature is our guide, regardless of how it seems at a particular moment.

Often, strong convictions are in opposition, because they don't fit every single situation, which is directly opposes our instincts. It is important to our lives that we learn the balance and different elements of what is natural and what is forced, because anything that is forced is not natural and is destined for destruction. For instance, we can't control change; but we can influence change by contributing to it. To attempt to be the sole controller of change is an example of what leads straight to destruction. The previous topic in the "The Process" chapter is another example.

Furthermore, when we contribute and oppose the attempt to control change, it all works out in a harmonious sequence. Why does this happen? Simply because there are unseen or unwritten laws that govern our existence, but we are ignorant to them. Sometimes we are instinctively obedient to them, resulting in our lives being eternally and internally blissful.

Short Demonstrations: Nature's Course

"Dad, what age did I start talking?"

"Well, I think you said your very first word at six months?"

"What word was that?"

"What do you think? It was *momma boy*, get it? *Momma boy*. Ha ha ha ha ha ha."

"Very funny, Dad! In comparison with my siblings, who spoke first?"

"Your sister spoke her first word at about four months old, and it was *no*."

"Wow! It seems to be that is her favorite word still!"

"Yes, you are correct, son."

"Dad, I ask because your grandson is now eight months old and is not talking much. It's kind of bothering me."

Why is it bothering you? My grandson is his own person. He is not you as you are not me. Please let him be."

But, Dad, I think that I should enroll my son into an early intervention speech therapy program for babies."

"Are you kidding me!"

"No, Dad, I am very serious. Michelle and I have spoken about it, and we even started interviewing some of the best therapist in the field. Dad, we want the best for our son."

"Good for you, son, but the fact of the matter is that you and Michelle are not giving my grandson a chance to develop naturally."

"But, Dad, everyone else's children in John's age group are already talking."

"Are you in a competition of some sort?"

"No, Dad, but we just want our son to be normal."

"What makes my grandson not normal, John, because he's quiet? That may also mean that he is a thinking man."

"Please don't get upset, Dad."

"Well, I am upset! You are going against the grain of nature by trying to force my grandchild to speak as you want and when you want him to. What bothers me most is you want him to talk before his time, then you go and sign him up for early intervention, which another term for baby's disability. He doesn't need this, John! Maybe I would understand if he was a bit older and did not say a word or acted weird. I love you, and I am always here for you as a father and often as a buddy, but I will not hear any more of this early intervention thing. Nature has a course, and we must respect nature's course because there are consequences when we don't. Often, we open a can of worms by forcing, rushing, and pushing nature to act as we would like it as oppose to working with nature. My last bit of advice is for you two to wait and see how he develops over the next several months. In the meantime, read to him, talk to him, and teach him what you want him to know. Assist nature in its course and do not force it to submit to your instant desire, then your life will be less stressful. Try it!"

WEALTHY PONDER

In order for rich people to get and maintain being rich they constantly think about material wealth, and they obtain it eventually. Some achieve their dreams and/or goals more abundantly than others. The same works for everything else in our lives, especially our mental and spiritual wealth.

In order for us to become spiritually and mentally wealthy, it is in our best interest to ponder an abundance of peace and positivity, which will create a balance to the challenges that life has to offer.

My wealth was traced to my desires, and according to Buddhist studies, "all of our suffering stems from our desires." In my opinion, when seeking harmony with existence, we start with our thought process first and then fill it with peace and positivity.

Take a moment to write how any of your suffering stems from your desires.

_____

_____

_____

_____

_____

_____

_____

_____

_____

_____

_____

_____

_____

_____

_____

_____

_____

_____

_____

_____

_____

_____

_____

_____

_____

_____

_____

_____

_____

_____

_____

_____

_____

_____

_____

_____

_____

_____

_____

_____

_____

_____

_____

_____

_____

_____

_____

MONITOR SELF

In order to maintain harmony with ourselves and our greater selves (the rest of the world; microcosm/macrocosm), we must acknowledge that it is in our best interest to monitor our thought patterns and deeds as often as possible. Monitoring ourselves is also a form of our mental and spiritual rejuvenation, through the experiences that we encounter and are naturally subject to.

Short Demonstration: Monitor Self

For instance, there was a young man who shared an apartment with his girlfriend. For the first time, he witnessed something that is a natural part of a woman's life in civilized societies.

The girlfriend was so comfortable with in their bond that she changed her sanitary napkin in his presence on one of her heavy days. The young man was amazed to learn about inner workings of the opposite sex. He was going through some spiritual turbulence, and on this particular day, it showed. The girlfriend, being herself, was just doing what she'd been doing for the last year and a half, and the young man verbally lashed out at her and said things that were really horrible to her.

"You are so disgusting! That is such a turnoff! What kind of woman does that in that manner?"

The girlfriend was bewildered, but out of survival, she fought back and argued that he did not feel that same way when they made love several days ago.

The young man left on bad terms with his girlfriend, and she just could not understand the sudden change in his attitude. As the day progressed, he felt guilty, began to do some introspection, and monitored his recent behavior in totality. Upon his conclusion, the he wondered how it got to that point of lashing out at his girlfriend when she was innocent. He declared to himself that he'd *monitor* himself on a daily basis the same way he'd monitor his computer for viruses.

Repeat these *titles* to yourself when needed and bear witness the power of the subconscious. We don't need a drink, a pill, a smoke, or any extrinsic substance to combat depression, anxiety, anger, fear, and other destructive thought patterns. We only need to channel our system of thought.

You have the option to use that free will and choose the power to say "Thank You" because "You Know Better," and you know the difference between "*I*-Reality and Reality." But always—and I mean always—pay close attention to "INTU." Now that we know better, let's do better because you now know better!

"Thank you for reading this great book!"

Best regards,

SHANTELL

www.ingramcontent.com/pod-product-compliance
Lightning Source LLC
Chambersburg PA
CBHW051552120626
46551CB00013B/1479